3 in 1 Social Media Guide Book

Table of Contents

Introduction..7

Chapter 1 Facebook Basics 9

Chapter 2 Creating a Facebook Profile or Page.............12

Chapter 3 What Type of Content to Post to Facebook ...19

Chapter 4 The Benefits of Facebook Groups 28

Chapter 5 The Use of Facebook Ads.............................36

Chapter 6 How to Direct Facebook Traffic to a Website51

Conclusion 54

Introduction..57

Legal Notes 60

Chapter 1. Instagram Marketing 61
Introduction to Instagram.......................................61
Tips To Growing Instagram Marketing. 62
Shooting Photos in a square mode: 62
Apply some strategic moves to bio links....................63
Cross-Promote...63
The Use of Trending Hashtags and Emoji That Calls For Action 64
Combination of Images and Videos 64
Sponsor ads..65
Use Valuable Content..65
Sponsor Post...66
Boomerang..66

Chapter 2. 67

How to PROMOTE AND DRIVE SALES ON
INSTAGRAM 67
A Well-Branded Instagram Profile............................67

Consistent Post 68

Ask Your Followers to "Tag Other Friends." 68

Learn to use the right filters 69

Be Responsive 69

Driving Traffic from Instagram 71

Exclusive Bonuses to Followers 71

Chapter 3. 72

Instagram Influencers (What Does This Mean?) 72

Benefits of Instagram Influencer 73

Tips to Choosing An Instagram Influencer: 73

Introduction to YouTube 78

IDENTIFY YOUR TARGET AUDIENCE 81

CREATE ORIGINAL 83

CONTENT ON A 83

REGULAR BASIS 83

FOLLOWING THE 86

EXAMPLES SET BY COMPANIES WITH ESTABLISHED
POPULAR YOUTUBE CHANNELS 86

RELATIVITY (Make your channel content relative to your
viewers) 89

SUPPORT CUSTOMER RESEARCH WITH KEYWORDS 91

SET A BUDGET 92

PROMOTION IS KEY 93

About The Author 95

"Facebook for Network Marketers:

Learn How to Increase Your Sales

Exponentially"

Harwood E. Jones

Email: midnightmediallc@gmail.com

Website: Midnight Media

"Facebook for Network Marketers: Learn How to Increase Your Sales Exponentially" © 2016 Harwood E. Jones

If you find yourself not doing anything in the next couple of minutes, go and review this book. I read all of the reviews and want to make more content to help with your needs.

Thank You!

Introduction

As a network marketer, when you wake up in the morning you may ask yourself how can you build better relationships with your clients or what you can do to build new relationships with potential clients. There are many ways to do this. Some are old school like being nice or speaking at events. These ways might still work, but the impact they have is reduced to a small number of listeners. Compared with the new methods the Internet era created, those ways are inefficient.

Online advertising, emails, websites and social media allow you to reach billions of people. You are no longer limited to people near you. When businesses are looking to have a global impact, they no longer waste money on old and inefficient ways.

One of the most effective social media for your business to have an impact among people is Facebook. It has the broadest range of options out there. Whether you are just starting out with network marketing or a giant MLM corporation, Facebook allows you to target a wide range of people. You can set up your Ads to target a small niche or the whole world population if needed. The opportunities are practically endless.

The social networking giant has more than 1.7 billion profiles. That means that your target audience probably has a Facebook profile.

In this book we will discuss the tools Facebook offers to engage your audience, how you can use Facebook strategically to target certain niches, what are Facebook Events and Groups and how to create them, how to direct Facebook traffic to your website, and ultimately make a sale. Although all of this might not look easy, after finishing this book you will have perfect knowledge and you will be able to reach millions of people that will be interested in your product.

<u>Why Facebook is so powerful?</u>

You may be use to sending direct emails to attract new customers. The problem with this is that you can't be absolutely sure that the person receiving the email will actually be interested in your business. Facebook lets marketers engage people in a new dimension.

With Facebook marketing, you can take advantage of your customers by them telling their friends through Facebook about your business. As you may know, word of mouth is really powerful in advertising. Also, Facebook is really powerful because it allows you to target people that are already talking about something related to your product or industry.

Facebook has billions of connected users, leveraging this connectivity lets you engage with people through creative content that will make your business stand out and lead to thousands of new clients for your product.

Chapter 1 Facebook Basics

Do you remember how your life was before Facebook existed? Maybe you used the Internet to send an email to a friend, or read about a certain topic. But, to keep up with your close social circle, you had to meet them for a talk or call them over the phone. With the creation of Facebook this changed forever. You are now able to keep up with a lot of people at the same time on one place. You now get updates of your friend being promoted or photos from your sister's baby all in your news feed. This is the power of Facebook. It helps keeping people connected.

What is Facebook?

Facebook is the most popular social network for connecting with people. Everything from status updates to personal photos is posted to Facebook and most of it is available for your friends to see (You can change your privacy settings to change this). You can send messages to any profile and chat. The site is available in more than 35 languages. It includes features such as:

1. Marketplace, which allows people to post, read and to answer classified Ads.
2. Groups, which allows people with common hobbies or interest to find each other and interact.
3. Events, which allow people to create an event, make it public and invite people.
4. Pages, which allows people to create a specific public page to promote a certain thing

Each personal profile contains a wall where friends can see your most recent posts, photos and videos. Also, they can post messages to your wall.

Facebook also has a News Feed which showcases real time interactions that occur between your friends, friends of friends and Pages. This can be used in favor of your business, because when someone comments something on your post, a real time update will be seen by everyone who has this "someone" as a friend. This makes networking much easier.

Facebook can be accessed through your phone and your pc.

Some Facebook Statistics

I will list some of Facebook's current statistics to help you visualize how big and helpful this social network is:

- 1.79 billion users, increasing over 15 percent year after year (Source: Facebook)
- 4.5 billion likes generated daily (Source: Facebook)
- Ages 25 to 34 dominates Facebook's demographics with 30 percent of the user base (Source: Emarketer 2012)
- Five new profiles are created every second (Source: ALLFacebook 2012)
- Highest traffic is from 1 to 3 PM (Source: Bit.ly blog)
- On Thursdays and Fridays traffic increases over 15 percent (Source: Bit.ly blog)
- 300 million photos a day (Source: Gizmodo)
- 4.75 billions of posts shared daily (Source: Facebook)

- **Every 60 seconds on Facebook: 510 comments are posted, 293,000 statuses are updated, and 136,000 photos are uploaded. (Source: The Social Skinny)**
- **Over 40 percent of Marketers report that Facebook is critical for their business (Source State of inbound Marketing)**

Do you see the impact you can achieve through using Facebook for marketing your product?

For example, let's say a popular local pastry shop doesn't use Facebook. They will be missing a lot. While many clients will talk about the local shop to a couple of people, many of its clients are taking pictures of the awesome looking pastries and posting them to Facebook. Most of the shop's customers and potential customers are using Facebook. So, it is therefore a must that the coffee shop creates its own Page where they can engage customers directly, comment on their photos, making offers to them and ultimately increasing the amount of people they impact. All of the new clients that the shop would lose if it hasn't created Facebook are too big. Then, the pastry shop can post updates saying things like: "Post photos of your pastries to Facebook this week for a chance of earning a dozen of pastries FREE". This is one of the ways Facebook can be used.

An example more related to network marketing is someone who sells let's say Avon products in a certain state. Using Facebook, he/she will be able to set up Ads for people who are interested in this industry, as well as setting up a radius of 20 miles for the Ad to show up. The Ad will only appear to people that are really potential customers. By doing this he /she now has thousands of soon-to-be clients that might contact him and buy his/her product. We will expand more on this in Chapter 4.

According to Zephoria.com, Facebook user base is growing by approximately 15 percent every year. Emarketer also affirmed that over 15 percent of adults search Facebook before purchasing something. This means that having a good Facebook Page might potentially make or break a sale decision. Developing a business Page is certainly essential for network marketing and really **any** business.

Chapter 1 Key Points:

- Facebook connects more than 1.5 billion people. Your target market is absolutely using Facebook daily.
- By not using Facebook to promote your business, you are losing a lot of potential customers.
- Network marketers can really benefit a lot from Facebook. You can really expect to increase your sales by a huge number. Your number of connections will increase exponentially.

Chapter 2 Creating a Facebook Profile or Page

Should I Create a Profile or a Page?

If you are a network marketer and just starting out with social media marketing, you might have asked yourself this very question. In the following paragraphs, I will try to explain the differences in the best possible way.

The main difference between a profile and a page in Facebook is that profiles are for personal, non-commercial use and represent a single person. When you use a profile and want people to be able to see your posts, you need them to add you as a friend. The main problem with this is that there is a limit to the amount of friends a profile may have (5000 friends). Once you reach this limit, people are able to follow your profile and be able to see your public updates. Some people may hesitate following a personal profile because it doesn't show the same level of professionalism a page offers.

Also, if you are going to represent a business, Pages are a must. You cannot use a personal profile to represent something that is not a person because it is against Facebook terms. Doing so may cause potential access loss to your account.

Pages are not that different to a profile in the way you post your public updates. Pages are handled by people with personal profiles. The good thing is that people can follow you in a much simpler way and there is no limit to the amount of people that can follow your updates. Following a page in Facebook is given the famous name of "Liking". When you like a page, you are basically following it. People that like a page will become your Page's fan. Fans will receive all the updates the Page posts in their news feed. Pages are specifically made for businesses, organizations and brands. They contain exclusive tools made to simplify all of the actions one would carry out when promoting his brand.

One of the features that allow you to have more control over your updates is called Page insights, where you are able to see stats like which posts are your fan's favorites and visitor demographics like location and age.

By using a Page, you can assign specific people to access and manage your Page by using Page roles. This person can edit your page the same way as you do.

And most importantly, by using a Page you can create Ads and boost posts. This will increase the amount of people that see the Page. These Ads will appear to people when they are reading their news feed in the sides of the website/App. We will expand more on the usage of Ads to expand your business in Chapter 4.

Before you create your page, here are some guidelines that will help you plan your way into a successful Page:

- Know your objective, how will you position yourself, and what Tone will you use in your posts.
- Fill out all the Page sections. Be sure to get images in the highest quality possible to set up as profile picture and cover photo. Include your website link so that people can get to your site.
- Be engaging with your audience. Your posts should be appealing and fun for your target audience. Your fans want to have a good time when reading their news feed. Try to encourage them to comment on your posts. And reply to all customers!
- Plan when you are going to share and what. There might be certain hours your target audience is more active. For example, if your target audience is kids you might want to schedule your posts for the most common lunch hours.

So to let this issue perfectly clear, I will give you some examples of Facebook Pages: Coca-Cola, Apple, Mashable, Nike, Oprah, Taylor Swift, New York Mets, Massachusetts Institute of Technology.

Setting up Your Page

Creating a page is really simple, you just have to go to www.facebook.com/pages/create and select the appropriate category for your page. The categories include: Local business or place; Company, Organization or Institution; Brand or Product; Artist, Band or Public Figure; Entertainment; And Cause or Community. If you are network marketing a certain product, you will need to choose either Local business; or Brand or Product.

If for some reason you have already created a personal profile to represent your business, Facebook allows you to convert your profile into a Page. This creates a new Facebook Page that's based on your personal account. This can be done only once. So pay attention in the future if you want to represent your business.

What will happen after you convert your Facebook profile into a Page?

- You will have a personal account and a Page
- Facebook will transfer your cover photo and profile picture to the Page
- The name of the profile will be shared
- You can access this new Page from within your personal account.

We have already seen why having a Facebook page is a must. But, if the Page is not set up correctly, it will be useless.

Designing a Facebook Page is really easy. Anyone can create his Page in some minutes, but it takes some planning and tinkering to make your Page right for business and to encourage its visitors to carry out a specific action. You, as network marketer might want to sell your product in a certain area or recruit more people to sell your product. By setting it up correctly, visitors will be much more receptive to your goals.

You will need to fill the most information you can. What should you be filling?

- Description: This will enable visitors to understand better the product you are selling. This is very similar to the "about" page you set up on your website. Having a good description can make or break someone liking your page and be interested in your product.
- Include your website if you have one, this might be useful for customers that want to become more informed on your product or if you are selling the product online.
- Profile picture: Here you have to add a good looking, attractive photo. It can be either a LOGO or a photo of your product. When you start using Ads people will see your profile picture in the Ad.
- Cover photo: Also really important. This photo is bigger and clients will see it on top of your Page. You will want a picture that really represents your business. Like, for example, a picture of your best sold product. Also, you can add text to your cover photo. You can include a call to action: "contact me today for 10% off in X product".

As we mentioned some couple of pages before, you can name different people to help you manage your page. This people can hold different levels of responsibility. I will show you the different positions and their responsibilities in the following chart:

	Manager	Content Creator	Moderator	Advertiser	Insight Analyst
Manage admin Roles	Yes	No	No	No	No
Edit the Page and add Apps	Yes	Yes	No	No	No
Create posts as the Page	Yes	Yes	No	No	No
Respond and delete comment	Yes	Yes	Yes	No	No
Send messages as the page	Yes	Yes	Yes	No	No
Create ads	Yes	Yes	Yes	Yes	No
View Insights	Yes	Yes	Yes	Yes	Yes

Chapter 2 Key Points

- Personal profiles are for personal, non-commercial use
- Pages are specifically made for businesses. They contain many tools that will help you engage your audience
- Pages are a must for anyone that wants to expand their business network
- Designing a page is easy. You just need some creativity

Chapter 3 What Type of Content to Post to Facebook

Now that your Facebook page is finally set up, you might ask yourself what is the main reason to post content to your Facebook Page. You are not sharing just to make your fans laugh. You should be posting to engage and ultimately grow a bigger audience. And at some point this audience will become your best clients.

When someone engages with your posts, be a like, a comment, or a share. You are growing your audience. Firstly, it means that your audience is enjoying the content you are posting and are probably recommending their friends to like your Page. Secondly, when a person likes or comments on your video, these actions appear on their friends' news feed: "[X person] has liked [or commented] on [Y Page post]". Both of these really increase your impact on people. Your page will become much better known.

Why do people use Facebook? They need to belong and they have a need for self-presentation. Most people log into Facebook to: Like content, message their friends, consume good content, comment status updates, and see what their friends are up to (Research by the Boston University).

Like vs. Share

When someone likes your post it means that they support the content you published. The content people share often means something to them, forging a bond with what they shared. When someone shares something, they are sharing it with probably their whole family, friends, colleagues and bosses. So when they share something it is because they agree strongly. Shares are much more valuable to your Page, because they increase your reach by a lot for free.

Different Types of Content

You might be wondering what content engages your audience the most. On the next pages, we will try to be clear on what the best content is and how to manage it.

There are different types of content you can post to your Facebook page. There are three main content categories you can post:

1. Images
2. Videos
3. Text

Images

Single Images Posts that include only one Image engage your audience 120 percent more than the average post. Photos engage your audience and are really easy to see and understand in a couple of seconds. They are the best content to post for marketing purposes. Images take up a large portion of your audience news feed; they draw much more attention than a simple text post.

Take a look on your Facebook news feed and see how much better a photo draws your attention than a text post, or thumbnail from a shared URL when you share a website's URL, Facebook displays a small thumbnail of it. If you want to share an URL you can just include it in your image posts. Use photos that are focused on what you want your audience to see. Images with a lot of contrast look great against Facebook's white news feed. For even better engaging include a short text that tells a story that your users can relate. Also, including text over your Image is great. You can include a call to action. For example: "Like this post," for one option, and, "Share it," for the other.

Good single images that are proven to engage your audience:

- Quotes: People love reading quotes from important people.
- Fun facts
- Comics/cartoons: Apart from making your audience laugh, some cartoons will inspire them to voice their opinion (AKA comment).

Photo Albums posts that include a photo album engage your audience 180 percent more than the average post. They are great to promote a new line of products, sponsor an event, and photo galleries of similar content. They allow posting multiple images of similar things without annoying your fans.

Goal: The main goal is to engage your audience in either them liking, commenting or sharing your Image.

Videos

Posts that include a video have twice as many engagements than the average post. When posting a video keep it simple and no longer than 2-3 minutes. They are great to show how to do something or events.

Goal: Same as the Image posts, video posts should engage your audience.

Text

Texts are best if they are short. They work best when they are approximately 250 characters (or 3 lines). They generate 60% more likes, shares and comments than texts longer than 250 characters. The best text posts are the ones that are interactive with your audience. Good examples include polls or questions. These types of posts generate more than 90 percent more engagement than the average text posts. Text key points:

1. No more than 250 characters
2. Call to action before the 100-character mark
3. Use a good Image to draw attention

Goal: With text only posts your aim should be to get people to comment and express their thoughts.

<u>Links</u>

Link posts happen when you paste a URL as a text post. Facebook generates a small thumbnail and description of the website for you. As I mentioned before, the thumbnail looks pretty small. It is better to post a photo because it looks much better. But if you need to include your website in a place other than the description of your Page or as a text in an Image content post, then this is the only option.

Goal: To increase traffic to your site. Your primary goal should be to get your audience to click and visit your website. The text should be short (no more than 150 characters) and include a call to action. For example: "Check out this website! Number 2 is my favorite. What is yours?" But be careful in including too much information because your reader won't need to check out the link because you gave them all the info.

<u>What other Type of Content Works for Business Pages?</u>

Other good content that really draws attention are promotions and discounts. For example: "Like, comment and share X post for a chance of winning Y product". To engage your audience even more you should set a specific deadline for them to check your promotion or discount. This creates a sense of urgency which will make them act even faster.

Reward your Facebook audience by including exclusive deals that only people who follow you on Facebook get. Your fans will feel special and they will probably recommend their friends to follow your Page so they can get the benefits.

You should relate your products to events that are happening in the world. For example: Christmas, Halloween, Thanksgiving, big financial events, etc. Your content can be tailored to the specific event. When close to Christmas, or Thanksgiving, if you post an image related to it or offer a special discount for the season, your audience will be much more engaged.

A good way to keep a constant flow of posts is to have a calendar with ideas for the content you will share with your audience. This content calendar will not only help you to publish regularly, but also it will guarantee that your content strategy is well thought out. Be interesting and keep up with events happening in the world. Look for a frequency that works for you and works for your fans.

Once you have the content calendar, Facebook Pages allows you to administer time better by setting up scheduled publications. To schedule publications, you just have to click the clock on the lower left corner of your Page. Schedule your content for when most of your fans are connected. You can find out about this see the Statistics of your Page.

Now that you know the content that most engages your audience, what should you do? You may choose to produce this kind of content by yourself and share it Facebook. That would be fine. But what would be even better is that before you share anything; learn what your audience wants. You might feel your audience wants certain kind of posts, but if these posts are not generating the right amount of engagement, then you might need to re-think your strategy. The best method to re-think your strategy is to make sure you know your audience, analyze your statistics and test different types of content.

Giveaways

Giveaways are really good to grow your audience. You post a good image of your product for example, and make people tag a friend and share the image. This is good at all growth stages, but works better when your Page is not too well known. It will attract a lot of people. Everyone will start tagging their friends. The growth is exponential. These giveaways, apart from growing your audience, will increase brand loyalty.

When someone gifts you something you are compelled to return the gift in the future. When a business gifts you something, the customer will want to reciprocate. He/she will want to buy the product in return. Think. What valuable can you give away that will trigger a "WOW that was really thoughtful"? This will trigger the effect of them being more loyal with your brand as well as probably buying you something in return.

Analyzing Your Facebook's Page Statistics

As we mentioned before, if you are looking for the best time to publish your content, the best place to find out is through Facebook Insight. A tool specifically designed for looking at your Page stats. In the next few paragraphs, we will discuss which insights you should consider the most.

When accessing the Insight tool, you will see many different tabs. The tabs divide the stats in different categories. They include: posts, videos, people and actions on Page.

The posts tab: You will discover two graphs that illustrate the average number of people who saw *any* content on Facebook by hour and day of the week. Pay attention to the "any" in the last sentence, as these stats don't show how many people actually saw your posts, but instead how many people are navigating Facebook at a given time. This tab will help you determine when the best time to publish your content is.

Also, there is another section in the posts tab that is very useful. It is called "All posts published" analytics. This section lets you check your posts in reverse chronological order and analyze each post engagement. Inside it there is tool called "Engagement rate" that helps you understand your post success by calculating the percentage of people who viewed and reacted to your post (liked, commented or shared). If your content is viewed by a large amount of people but it has a low Engagement rate, the post is marked as "Low quality". Having too many low quality posts hurts your Page because the algorithm that chooses which posts appear on your fans news feed is highly affected displaying less your posts.

Facebook has recently introduced a new way to react to content called "Reactions" which lets you know how people feel about your post. These reactions include being: wow, sad, angry, in love and ha-ha. Tracking reactions lets you know what your fans feel about your content.

Next, there is another section in the posts tabs called "Post Types". It shows which of your posts produced the highest engagement for your Page.

The videos tab displays the number of views your videos had, amount of people who watched your video more than 10 seconds and a list of your best videos.

The video stats can be filtered by:

- The ones that have been seen by people organically and the ones that have been seen by people because you paid to advertise it.
- The ones that were auto played vs. the ones that people click to see it.
- The ones that were played only once vs. the ones repeated.

The people tab you can go to "people engaged" to view the demographics of your audience categorized by the ones that liked your Page, the ones you have reached with Ads, and the ones engaged.

These analytics let you view your audience you engage sorted by location, age, gender, and language. Knowing who your main audience is really helps you to plan the type of content you will publish

The actions on Page tab: Recently Facebook added the possibility to add a call to action button. It has up to eleven different actions, like call the business or booking an appointment. This tab allows you find out the amount of people that clicked this button, the demographics and if they clicked it from their pc or from their Smartphone.

In conclusion, use Facebook Insights to your advantage in planning strategically the content you will publish.

Chapter 3 Key Points:

- When someone engages with your post, you are increasing your audience.
- People share content they deeply relate with.
- Keep your text post short and interactive.
- Images are the best type of content.
- Use Facebook Insights to plan strategically the content you will publish.

Chapter 4 The Benefits of Facebook Groups

You might be thinking whether if it's better to create a Page or Group. But in reality, you should be using both. Facebook Groups and Pages can be best friends if used correctly. Through both of them you can stay ten times more connected with your audience. A Facebook Group allows you to have next level communication with fans.

To understand how these two are tied, let's first explain the differences between them.

Differences between Facebook Groups and Pages

We have already explained thoroughly what Facebook Pages are. If you want information on what a Facebook Page is refer to Chapter 2. So let's continue with what Facebook Groups are.

Pages were designed to be profiles for businesses, celebrities, etc. They are formed by a huge number of people. As they are so big, one to one communication with the business is very hard. On the other hand, a Group is a place for small group communication where people who share a common interest express their opinions on a certain subject. People join a group because they share a common cause. These may be having an issue or activity to organize, discuss certain subjects or share related content.

Being a network marketer, you can create a Facebook Group around certain people who are near you and would like to sell your product for you. In it you discuss more private information and give knowledge to others. Then, you would have a Page of your product. In the group you discuss matters with the people who work for you and in the Page you advertise in order to make your product better known.

Setting up Your Group's Privacy Settings

When you create a Facebook Group you are given the option to choose between it being Public, Private or Secret. In the following chart you will understand what each of these categories entitles.

Who can…?	Public	Private	Secret
Join	Anyone can join or be added by a current member	Anyone can ask to join or be added by an admin	Anyone, but they have to be added either by a current member or an admin
See the group's name	Anyone	Anyone	Members and former members
See who the group members are	Anyone	Anyone	Members only
Stories about the group on Facebook's news feed	Anyone	Members only	Members only
See the group's description	Anyone	Anyone	Members and former members
See the group's tags	Anyone	Anyone	Members and former members

See what members post in the group	Anyone	Members only	Members only
Find the group in search	Anyone	Anyone	Members and former members

Facebook Groups in Business

As we said, using Facebook Groups alongside your Page is highly beneficial to achieve much better communication with your audience. In business, this is essential to achieve the ultimate goal of increasing and building relationships with people.

Groups let you set up a cover photo which will reflect your business brand. Admins can change this with letting Facebook set it up for you with an image of all the profile photos of your group's members.

Unlike Pages, Groups have a feature that lets you and your members search for previous post. So if someone is asking a commonly asked question, you can tell them to search for previous posts discussing the same issue. The results that the search shows are posts that contain the given words in any part of it. The given words will be highlighted so they are easily found.

Some of the tools that Groups contain are:

- Events
- Files (you can upload or create any type of file)

- Notifications

The tools may come handy, but they are not the main reason you are using Groups for Business.

Reasons to use Groups in Business

1. Gather people who have similar interests

All of us really like to be with people who share common interests, right?

If your business offers a certain product or service, these products or services might have lots of people who want to discuss between themselves about them. For example, in the case of Network Marketing, there might be a "Herbalife" group where people might have doubts about the different protein tastes or why are they healthy products. All of these questions might arise and encourage conversation between people. A group is the best place to hold these types of conversations. You can answer their questions and let other people contribute too.

Why is it beneficial for business? As conversations become more interesting, members might want to invite their friends to the Group. This translates into new possible clients or brand ambassadors to do the talking for you.

2. Become "friends" with brand ambassadors

Every business has loyal clients who love telling their friends about how great your product or service is. This people are called brand ambassadors. Giving them power to do the talking is really smart. You now have free advertisement, as well as testimonials for your product or service.

Dialogue within a Group will help you strengthen this connection between these loyal clients and you.

Also, for network marketing, groups are really great to communicate with people who want to sell your product. You can help your salespeople or discuss new ideas.

Why is it beneficial for business? Your brand ambassadors will now have a tool that reaches large amounts of people to tell your story.

3.   Discuss new ideas with salespeople

You can discuss new ideas, help, and ask for your salespeople input through Groups. A good leader can create a Facebook group to promote new ideas and gain support.

Why is it beneficial for business? You can forge better relationships with your committee.

4.   Easier to be seen in the news feed

When people join a group, they know that what is being discussed is relevant to them. It is easy to know as they joined because they wanted and can leave when they want to. Your audience wants to be personally connected to what is being discussed in Groups. Also, group members are more likely to see the posts because they receive a notification each time a new post is published; and if they have commented on a post each time someone comments, they will receive a new notification.

Why is it beneficial for your business? Better communication with your audience and salespeople.

5.   Members are more willing to give their personal contact info

One of the main goals of using Facebook for marketing is to enhance your relationships with old and new clients. Are you trying to build your first email list? Using a Facebook Group is a good way to achieve this naturally.

One of the ways is to propose events or activities that require their email to sign up. Or you might ask for someone's email to discuss a more private matter. All of these are ways to get people onto your mail list.

People are much more predisposed to share their email, phone number or any other private information as they feel that in a group everyone knows each other and it's a safe place to do so.

Why is it beneficial for your business? Having more personal relationships with your customers enables you to:

- Receive better feedback from your clients.
- Add them to your email list, being able to send them relevant news on your products or services.
- Create even more brand ambassadors.

6.   You can sell products through Facebook groups

In addition, from being a great communication tool, Facebook Groups allow you to use them as a marketplace. You can post products for sale in it like in any other online marketplace. You can set its price, location, description and add photos.

<u>Why is it beneficial for your business?</u> You now have an additional place to sell your product/service. If the Group turns out to have a lot of members, you can sell a lot through it.

7.   If you are a network marketer, you can add video training courses.

You might want your salespeople to watch certain educational videos that will help them and you make more sales. This can easily be shared within the Group's file system. They will be stored forever and can be easily referenced whenever you want to. With the option of keeping your Group secret, you can be sure this content is watched only by the people you want.

<u>Why is it beneficial for your business?</u> Your salespeople will have an easy way to instruct themselves and will result in more sales.

8.   Establish expertise

By answering all of the questions people might have, you declare yourself someone who really knows what you are doing. When you help other you always receive back. Try to give the most amount of value you can.

<u>Why is it beneficial for your business?</u> You will be sure that people know you are knowledgeable in your product/service and its benefits. You can destroy your competition by doing this as you will be known as the best of certain field.

9.   You now have a core following of people who trust you.

Let's say you have a thousand members in your Group, you now have a following! This is great for any business. You now have good feedback always. You had a new idea? You can see how a sample of people reacts. Do you want to launch a new product or service? These people trust you and will probably buy from you as soon as the product/service launches.

Why is it beneficial for your business? It is pretty clear why having a following is great for business, right? You now have a network of people!

Now that you know how helpful having a Business Group is, the only thing you need to do is being consistent in engaging with your members. This alone will set things in motion to achieve whatever your goal is. Try to encourage good discussions that you can contribute a lot. To not only provide value, but to show your expertise.

Chapter 4 Key Points

- You should have a Facebook Page AND a Facebook Group
- Facebook Groups allow you to communicate better with your audience
- Groups will help you and consolidate your business among your competition
- Groups will build you a following

Chapter 5 The Use of Facebook Ads

There are more than 1.5 billion people using Facebook. It has people from everywhere in the world, people who will be interested in your product or service and are actively looking for it. Sometimes these people who are actively searching for your products will need some extra help in finding your product or service. Others might still not know they are searching for something like your product or service. With the help of Facebook Ads, you can target these specific people. These, and only these, will see your Ads. Only the people who you know that can be interested. That is why Facebook Ads are one of the best out there: because they can be targeted to certain demographics!

Some of you may have a friend who keeps insisting that Facebook Ads do not work. They are probably saying this because they have read an article of someone who used Facebook Ads to promote his business and failed miserably. But, he probably was doing it wrong. Why were there over one million advertisers who spend more than eight billion dollars on Facebook Ads then? Since 2010, Facebook advertising has grown over 650 percent! There is a reason for these. In this Chapter you will learn how to properly use Facebook Ads.

Difference between Facebook Ads and Google AdWords

The main difference between the two is that using Google AdWords limits your product or service to people who are actively searching for it. They search for a keyword using Google search and your advertised page appears on highlighted on the top.

Firstly, there are a limited numbers of keywords you may enter in Google AdWords. What are keywords?

Keywords are words people might search for. For example, let's say you search for "Hotels in Barcelona", Google will give you lists of pages who will help you book a Hotel in Barcelona. But, you want your Website to stand out. So, you pay Google to position your Website on the top.

Secondly, as I said, they are not targeted. People who have an interest won't just stumble upon your website. They need to search for it. And if you are lucky to have a product that a lot of people are searching for, then it might be worth it. But, if your product is something new, and innovating that people still don't have a clue about, Facebook Ads are much better: They are targeted for people who already might have an interest in you.

Facebook Ads are also getting better every year. Just a couple of months ago they introduced new features for targeting your audience even better.

Facebook recently acquired Instagram, so now Ads are stronger than ever. Your Facebook Ads will also show on people Instagram's feed. Your audience is now bigger!

So, are you convinced to use Facebook Ads for your business yet?

Some Definitions

Ad campaign: A Campaign consists of one or more Ad sets or Ads. You can choose the main objective for your campaign. You should create a campaign for each different objective.

Ad sets: Ad sets consist of one or more Ads. You can define your target audience, budget, schedule and placement. You should organize each of your Ad sets to target your audience.

Ads: The actual Advertisement for your product or service.

<u>Setting up Your Facebook Ads Account</u>

Now, you will learn how to setup your Facebook advertising account. You will also learn how to handle permissions, changing and knowing your spending limit and other useful information that will help you plan your Ads strategically.

The first thing you need to set up is your payment method. Facebook allows most credit cards, PayPal. Fill in all the information asked when setting up the Ad account settings. If you are from Europe, Facebook will ask you to fill in your vat information. You can also set up the currency you want to be billed in and your time zone. Be extra careful when filling this page as this information can't be changed in the future.

I suggest you to add a second payment method as well, because if for some reason your primary payment method fails, for example if your credit card reaches the monthly limit, your Ads will be paused until you can pay for them. Restarting them can be a boring process.

In the past, Facebook charged your payment method each time someone clicked your Ad. Now, Facebook introduced changes that you reach certain thresholds and you are charged each time you reach that amount. The amount your threshold can be varies depending for how long you have been using Facebook Ads. You will first start with a $25 threshold; you will be billed $25 each time you spend $25 on your Ads. As your payments are processed correctly, this threshold will increase in intervals to $50, $250, $500 up to $750.

Having a higher threshold doesn't affect your Ads. It just changes the amount of times you will be billed for the Ads so that your payment method invoice is shorter.

Facebook Ads have limits. Regularly this won't be an issue, but it is better to have the knowledge and possibly expect it and, ultimately, know how to solve it. The limits are:

1. 5000 Ads per account.
2. 1000 campaigns per account
3. 25 advertisement account per user.

If for some reason you reach any of these limits, all you have to do is delete your old Ads and campaigns.

Also, there existed a limit that set the maximum amount of money you could spend on your Ads daily. But with the introduction of thresholds, this limit has been removed.

There exists another limit that YOU can set. It is a limit that that totals the amount of money you want to spend in Facebook Ads for your account. By default, it is set to be unlimited. But, if for some reason you wish to limit it you can manage it from the "billing" page.

Another important thing to set up is the notifications you receive. You should always be checking how your Ad campaigns are performing. Receiving notifications is a great way to stay informed. But if they are set incorrectly they can flood your inbox! Changing notification settings is a must. In your account information you will find two sets of notifications triggers: One for your email and the other one for your In-Facebook notifications. Simply check or uncheck the boxes. You should disable the "Ad approved" notification as those can really flood your inbox; you should only receive the ones that notify you when your Ads are rejected. Set your notifications to receive the most important ones to your email and the least important ones to your In-Facebook notifications.

Ad Types for Each Objective

There are many different types of Ads you can create in Facebook. Before creating your first campaign, I will explain to you the different Ads available. Throughout all these years, Facebook has really adjusted its advertisement; no matter what you want to advertise, you will find the correct type of Ad for it!

Increasing Your Website's Traffic Ads

One of the purposes of creating a Facebook Ad is to deliver traffic to your website. This has the goal to get people to visit a certain landing page where they can buy your products, subscribe to your email list, etc.; or just increase your site's audience.

These are the Ads you will want to use for getting people to visit your website:

Domain Ad these Ads are placed on the Facebook's right column, so it is not available for mobile users. This is one of the simplest Ads you can create. In this Ad you can set up a title, a short description and the link to be displayed. Statistically, it underperforms in terms of its click-through rate (CTR), but if you are short on budget it's a good Ad to have as they are the cheapest.

Page Post Link these Ads are placed on Facebook's right column or on your audience news feed. Also, they are supported in mobile devices and desktop. It's the most commonly used Ad type. It's the best Ad type for promoting your website. These Ads consist of a big image that catches your audience attention (pick a good, high-contrast image) and a small description where you can explain what your product or service is all about. Statistically, these Ads perform really well. They also have the nifty side benefit of generating likes for your Facebook Page. A good way to increase the Ad's impact is to reply to the comments your audience leaves.

Increasing Sales and Leads for your Business Ads

If you want to advertise an e-commerce stores or a brand, Facebook allows you to show multiple products or services in the same single Ad.

Facebook has also an Ad where people can leave their email addresses without leaving Facebook itself. This is just plain awesome. People are much more convinced on leaving their email through Facebook than if they have to visit an "outside" website. The credibility is much higher also.

Multi-Product (Carousel): These ads appear on your audience's news feed. They are supported for people using their mobile devices or desktop. It was released on mid 2014. They are very useful for marketers looking to advertise multiple products or services at the same time. You can include up to five images each of them with a different title and one short description. For example, if you own a MLM where you sell multiple tableware objects, using this type of Ad is beneficial because you are able to showcase five of your objects at the same time on the same Ad.

Dynamic Product Ads (DPA): These Ads appear on Facebook's right column or on your audience news feed. They show on desktop and on mobile. They also consist of a big image and a title. But, these Ads are one of the best because they automatically target the people that might be interested in your product or service. They check on people past actions (cookies) and if they have searched for something related to your business, these Ads will show up automatically in their Facebook.

Lead Ads: These Ads are available both for desktop and mobile. They were introduced in 2015. These Ads are really awesome for getting people emails right inside Facebook. They also consist on an image, a title and a short description. When your audience clicks on the Ad a form pops up right there. People do not need to leave Facebook and visit an external website to sign up to your newsletter, for example. As you might have guessed, these Ads are great for lead generation.

Canvas: These ads are mobile only. Basically, they are *interactive* Ads. That is why they are only available in mobile devices. They look like a regular Ad with an image, title and short description. But, when someone clicks them they open a Canvas where can swipe, tilt, zoom in and out images. They are completely different in this sense than other Ads.

Engagement for your Page Ads

Whether your goal is promoting your business Page or promoting your existing Page posts to reach more people, Facebook Ads are a great way to do so. There are Ads specifically designed to issue the latter goals. Anyways, in all cases it is important to target the right audience.

Page Like These Ads are the best for solely increasing your Page likes. They appear on the right column or on the news feed and are available in both Desktop and Mobile. It features a big image with a short description. But, most importantly it features a highly visible call-to-action for user to like your Page by clicking the Ad. As always, it is very important to pick an image that will catch your target audience eye.

Page Post Photo These Ads are also featured on the right column or on your audience news feed. These Ads appear only to people who have liked your Page, so keep that in mind. They are available in both Desktop and Mobile. This Ad features the biggest space of them all. It has a huge space for a nice image as well as short description. If you pick the right image people will be engaging like crazy.

Page Post Video These Ads are similar to Page Post Photo Ads. The difference is that the promoted content is a video. Statistically, videos are the most engaging content of all. So if you can produce a great video that connects with your business principles, plus connecting with your audiences' you will get exceptional engagement rates.

Page Post Text I am just going to mention these types of Ads. In my opinion there is no reason to promote a text post as promoting a Page Post Photo drives much more engagement and is ultimately much more worth your money.

Installs for Mobile Apps Ads

These Ads are beneficial if you are using some kind of app to promote your MLM. If you are not using an app, skip this part because the goal of these Ads is to get installs for it.

Mobile App these Ads are really similar to the Page Like Ads in terms of how they look, but instead of having a CTA to like your page, they have a CTA button to install an app. They are only available for Mobile users. When using these Ads, you will be able to choose if you want them to appear on devices with iOS, Android or both; if you want to target people using tablets; and if you want to target people that are using WIFI.

Visitors for Your Event or Store Ads

The goal of these Ads is to lead people to your physical store or event. The results are hard to measure because they are offline. If used correctly, they can be successful.

Offer: These Ads appear on the right column or on the news feed, are available for both Desktop and Mobile. These are perfect for people who want to attract other people to their stores. It features a picture and short description. Plus, a call to action button that lets your audience get an offer to redeem personally on your store. If you can tailor your target audience to people near you that are interested in your business, you will get great results!

Event: These Ads appear on the right column or on the news feed, they are available for both Desktop and Mobile. Facebook events are awesome for organizers who want to attract visitors. If you want to increase the reach of your event these Ads are absolutely helpful. Remember to limit the geographical reach of the Ad to people near you.

As we are learning, Facebook has a different type of Ad for each goal you or your business might have. Pick strategically and don't be afraid to experiment and, using Ads statistics, determine which type of Ad is best.

<u>Setting up Your First Ad</u>

Now you are fully knowledgeable in setting up your first Ad account and the different Ad types that Facebook offers. What to do next? It is time to create your first Facebook Ad. Before even paying a dollar, you should have a clear purpose or goal to achieve with this Ad campaign. Think about this and once you have decided the purpose head to Facebook Ads Manager and click "create an Ad" button.

The first thing that Facebook asks you is what goal you want to achieve with your Ad. Here you will have a list which will include every different Ad type we have seen in the last paragraphs. If you are promoting your website, statistically, choosing Website conversions yields much better results than Website clicks.

Now that you have determined your Ad campaign type, you will be asked to select up to six different images. Be sure to at least include three different images to test different Ad variations, you should use A/B approach. Do not be afraid to test. Use big, eye catching images. Images are what increase your audience engagement the most.

You can choose three different methods to upload an image: you can upload an image from your PC, re-use a previously used Image, or browse images in Shutterstock (This is great if you want to keep things on the cheap side and find a high-quality picture, though if you want your Ad to be unique I would get my own pictures.)

Once you set up your image, you will be asked to set up the Ad's copy. This is probably the trickiest part of setting up your Ad. Choosing the right words can bare a HUGE increase in engagement. Choose them wrong and your Ad will fail. Be sure to include the benefits of your product or service. Make people know how your product will help them. Provide value. You need to write copy for the title (25 characters long), description (90 characters) and news feed URL description (90 characters). As with the image, having different copy variations is really good. Test out! If you can offer a discount or something of the sort it is great to increase the amount of clicks you will get.

Ok, you now have your copy and image set up. You only need to determine the best placement for your Ad. You can choose between Mobile, right column, or news feed.

Statistically, news feed Ads perform the best. However, as right column Ads are much cheaper, you can test out how well they perform.

Another thing to have in mind when choosing Mobile is to be careful to not lead the people clicking your Ad to a non-Mobile website. Otherwise you will have thrown your money down the toilet.

Determining Your Target Audience

This might be the most crucial step of creating your Ads. If you target your Ads wrongly you will get the wrong likes, "Cheap Likes", even if you get thousands of likes. You will not sell the same amount than if you target the correct audience. Also, the engagement rate will be much slower.

Demographic Ad Targeting

This way of targeting your Ads is the simplest out there. It is a pretty straight forward process. You will be able to choose between:

- **Location:** From country to zip codes. Be careful what you choose here. Depending what your product or service is and how much you want to spend you can choose the whole world or a "near you" ten-mile radius. Be wary that if you choose a large area you will get a lot of likes but it will be much more expensive. If you are promoting a coffee shop, you should target to a small radius near you. If you are offering a product that can be delivered anywhere in the US, choosing the whole US is a good idea as long as you can handle the costs.
- **Age:** Depending what your product or service is, you should choose between teenagers, young adults, people with families or retired people.

- **Gender:** When choosing gender, target specific genders. Nowadays, Facebook offers a huge selection of different genders. Up to fifty different ones! You can target different audiences depending what your product is. Be sure to change the copy and images for different genders. Males, for example, should be approached different than women.

Recently, Facebook added the option to pick your target audience even more specifically. You can set to target with people with certain political views, job titles, ethnicity, etc. When choosing your target be wary that some people might not have filled this type of information in your profile. You might end up narrowing your audience too much.

Interest Ad Targeting

This type of Ad targeting is the best one to use. It allows you to target people who are interested in your product or service particularly. For example, you can target people who are interested in your competitor's product or your market.

You will be able to choose between:

- **Precise Interests:** This type of targeting lets you target people based off their profile information. This targeting keeps targets people who have liked something related to your industry. Facebook will let you type different industries. Once you select the most appropriate one, Facebook will show you a list of other related industries you can add. Add more than one interest so that you don't narrow your audience too much.
- **Behavior targeting:** Facebook analyzes each profile actions using cookies. If

someone is looking for protein powders and then uses Facebook, he will probably get protein powders Ads. It does not always work great, but if it does it's the best. You are sure that people who see your Ad are actively interested in something similar to your product or service.

Connection Ad Targeting

This type of Ad targeting looks for people who already like your Page, who are friends with people who have liked your Page or people who have not liked your Facebook Page.

You can use this type of targeting, for example, if you have a Page with millions of likes and want to engage people who have not liked your page yet, Connection Ad Targeting is awesome.

You can also increase the engagement of your Page posts by targeting people who are friends with your "likers".

Custom Audience Ad Targeting

This may be the most powerful Ad targeting if you have a list of emails, phone numbers or profile IDs. This way you can now that the Ads will show to people who you know that have given you their information because they are interested. By using this way of targeting you can up sell new products, make newsletter subscribers clients, etc.

If used correctly, this targeting method will yield the highest conversion rate. For example, if you are focusing on lead generation or people subscribing to your newsletter, you can exclude people who you already have their email.

Analyzing How Successful your Ad Campaign Is

Once your Ad is already out there, you can check out how it is performing using Facebook Ad Manager. Here, you will be shown statistics of people who have clicked your Ad, how much each click costs, the whole campaign reach, the amount of money spent today, total amount of money spent so far, start and end date.

As you can see these statistics are pretty specific. You can analyze lots of things from these campaign stats. If you want to understand how your campaign is performing today, be sure to select stats from the last seven days! Otherwise, your metric and recent results will be harder to measure and understand.

Analyzing each campaign is easy: you just need to click on the list shown in Facebook Ad Manager. Here you can disable the campaign for a while, view click frequency and view the clicks over time your Ads received in a graph. The FREQUENCY of your campaign is really important to pay attention to. It tells you how many times a unique user has seen your Advertisement. It is important to analyze because the higher the number, the less eye catching your ad is. The user saw your Ad, let's say, fifteen times until he clicked on it. Ultimately, your costs will go up and the results will go down!

Chapter 5 Key Points

- Make your Ads pop with nice looking, eye-catching images.
- Craft your Ads copy attentively.
- Don't be afraid to test different Ad variations.
- Before creating any type of Ad you need to be sure about its purpose it will have so you can determine the Ad type you will use and the way to target it.

- Analyze your campaign statistics, change the Ad accordingly. Pay attention to the **Frequency** stat.

Chapter 6 How to Direct Facebook Traffic to a Website

In the last chapter we have seen how to drive traffic to your website using Ads. But, also, there are other ways to achieve an increase in your website's traffic. In this chapter you will learn different techniques to achieve higher website traffic through Facebook. Are you ready?

Make Sure Your Website is Updated Regularly with New Content

Imagine that someone enters a website you have linked through Facebook and all they can find is a bad looking landing page, that doesn't show the website's purpose, while showing posts from two years ago. People will just leave the page without even reading anything. And sure that they won't share the page with their friends, or comment on your posts about it. Be sure to post something useful at least once a week. Some ideas that might help you with coming up with new content are:

1. Post a tip about your niche weekly. It doesn't have to be too long. Just a couple of paragraphs and a nice looking image. Try to answer some questions that your customers might have about your service or product.

2. Post an article of top 10 articles about something related to your business. You can find them all around the web. You can even add a short paragraph describing what you liked about each article.

3. Post an interview with someone related to your niche. The interview can just be 5-10 questions you have sent the interviewee through your email account.

Not only this will benefit in driving more traffic from Google keyword (search engine indexing), but it will encourage people to subscribe to your newsletter and be more excited about your Facebook Page posts.

Make it Easy to Share Your Website's Content to Facebook

People reading your content might want to share your articles to Facebook. This will increase traffic as, basically, you are getting free advertisement. Their friends will see the content they have shared and probably will surf your website.

To do this you need to add Facebook share button to your website. Be sure to include it in a place where it is viewable and in every single article you publish. Make it simple.

Another way for making your website readers share your content to their Facebook is just reminding them at the end of your articles! For example, "Did you like this article? Feel free to share it to Facebook by just clicking the button below!"

Optimizing Your Facebook Profile

Make sure you include your website's link in other places of your Page. For example, in the About Us page of your Facebook Page, include different links to different sections of your website. You might describe what your product or service is about including your website's link where they can read further. "Our product offers porcelain tableware at the best market prices. Find out more at www.yourwebsite.com/moreinfo

Chapter 6 Key Points

- Don't be afraid to think out of the box, post your website's URL everywhere you can. Ads are not the only way to drive more traffic.
- Keep your website updated and include a share to Facebook button.

Conclusion

Congratulations! You now have the knowledge to start building and increasing your business' clients. Eventually, the use of Facebook will increase your sales exponentially. Remember to not be afraid to test different variations in everything: your Page, your Ad campaigns and your Group. Although my recommendations of what works better statistically varies, different businesses might get more benefits using other type of Ads.

Make your content interesting, don't act like a robot. Your clients are people with feelings. Remember this and put it into action. Think what you would like to see if you where on your customers' feed. What value does your product or service provide? What is in it for them? List your product or service benefits and be sure to let your customers know what they are.

As a network marketer, remember what your new salespeople or new clients want. If you were someone who wants to start selling for a network marketing business, what would you want to know? Probably you would be seeking for a company you can trust, a person you can look up to, testimonials, and make money. Think of these things and include them in your Ads, Page, Groups and Website. If you were a client, you would be seeking what most people look for: how valuable is the product or service? People are willing to take out their VISA if they see that your product or service can solve something for them, make them look prettier, etc.

I want you to pay attention to this psychological study which found out how human beings are programmed, in terms of what they desire. Called Life Force Eight, the desires are the following:

1. Survival, enjoyment of life, life extension.

2. Enjoyment of food and beverages.

3. Freedom from fear, pain, and danger.

4. Sexual companionship.

5. Comfortable living conditions.

6. To be superior, winning, keeping up with the Joneses.

7. Care and protection of loved ones.

8. Social approval.

Make sure everything you create appeals to this desires.

Take Action, Provide Value, And Earn Money!

INSTAGRAM MARKETING

INSTAGRAM MARKETING TIPS TO HELP MOVE BUSINESSES TO THE NEXT LEVEL

By

HARWOOD E. JONES

Copyright © 2017

Email: midnightmediallc@gmail.com

Website: Midnight Media

Introduction

With over 600 million monthly users, Instagram continues to be a growing platform. New features are always arriving, continuing to make the app more engaging to its users. The support from Facebook, in my belief, will allow Instagram to stay around as long as Facebook will become the next best way to engage with a larger audience.

What you will learn from Instagram Marketing:

- Simple tricks to grow your Instagram Account
- How to promote sales across the platform
- How to get more interactions with potential customers
- How filters can increase engagement
- To drive traffic to an outside website or online store
- Use of Influencer Marketing
- A formula to determine overall engagement and growth

Table of Contents

Introduction

Table of Contents

Legal Notes

Chapter 1. Instagram Marketing

Introduction to Instagram
Tips To Growing Instagram Marketing.
Shooting Photos in a square mode:
Apply some strategic moves to bio links
Cross-Promote
The Use of Trending Hashtags and Emoji That Calls For Action
Combination of Images and Videos
Sponsor ads
Use Valuable Content
Sponsor Post
Boomerang

Chapter 2.

How to PROMOTE AND DRIVE SALES ON INSTAGRAM

A Well-Branded Instagram Profile
Consistent Post
Ask Your Followers to "Tag Other Friends."
Learn to use the right filters
Be Responsive
Driving Traffic from Instagram
Exclusive Bonuses to Followers

Chapter 3.

Instagram Influencers (What Does This Mean?)

Benefits of Instagram Influencer

Tips to Choosing An Instagram Influencer:

About The Author

Other Books By Harwood Jones

Can I Ask A Favor?

Legal Notes

No part of this publication may be reproduced, distributed, or transmitted in any form or by any means, including photocopying, recording, or other electronic or mechanical methods, or by any information storage and retrieval system without the prior written permission of the publisher, except in the case of very brief quotations embodied in critical reviews and certain other noncommercial uses permitted by copyright law.

Introduction to Instagram

Instagram has been the largest mobile photo sharing app for over 6 years and was initially owned by Burbn Inc. It was created by Kevin Systrom and Mike Krieger and launched in 2010. This social media network was acquired by Facebook in April 2012 for about a billion dollars in cash. Instagram has grown to be the widest social media network so far.

As of 2013, Instagram increased by 23% while the parent company Facebook only rose by 3%. In June 2013, it was enabled to support videos, allowing users to watch video contents through it. It could only allow uploads of pre-recorded standard definition clips of about 15 seconds. Later, updates increased the time limit for recorded files. Instagram has been equipped with excellent filters that can give a photo an entirely different look. Instagram has really inspired a lot of social media users, thereby doing business on it.

In 2016, Instagram launched what is called Instagram Stories. Instagram Stories lets users share photos and videos, which would vanish after 24 hours and does not appear on the user's Instagram feeds. Later on, Instagram moved to the live video feature, thereby giving the user an opportunity to make a video live and allowing users to stream them live.

The great photo-sharing app is simple and is growing everyday. Instagram has nearly 400 million daily users and great user engament. But the most under utilized feature Instagram offers is to be used as an avenue to market their business and make money from it.

Instagram is a platform used majorily for sharing photos and videos and to also do other social activities. Instagram gives its users access to taking snapshots and making a video in public or in private with the use of the application, and can also share them on other social media platforms such as Facebook, Twitter, Tumblr, and Snapchat. Instagram is one of the fastest-growing platforms in the world and has made a significant impact in the society of today. Majority of businesses are very eager to make their presence known and engage with potential customers on the network.

Tips To Growing Instagram Marketing.

Shooting Photos in a square mode:

Instagram feed is full of different photos and videos, so you need to start with uploading some high-quality photos to help your marketing on Instagram more efficient. Taking squared photo is one of the best ways to get a better photo for Instagram and likewise save time. Most cameras have this mode built-in their settings and smartphones also have their way of setting this mode up too.

The square mode saves you the time of cropping photos before you upload them. It ensures that the photos are resized in such a way that the essential message you're trying to pass across to the viewers is not entirely cropped out. You could as well get applications that are known for things like this, because the Instagram app has some limitation when it comes to shooting photos. Using third party apps, you can take some extremely high-quality photos.

These apps include and are not limited to:

- Snapseed
- VSCO
- Lumyer
- Parfait

Your Google Play Store and iOS App Store have endlessly many possibilities.

Apply some strategic moves to bio links

Using Instagram is fun, but making Instagram a marketing tool is a little bit more calculating. You need to plan the posts you intend to make ahead of time. For small business owners, who wish to establish themselves on Instagram, put the link in your bio to a landing page that has the same posts like the one posted on Instagram. This way you can take the lead in promoting your blogs, e-commerce websites, gain more subscribers, etc.

Cross-Promote

You can Cross-brand whenever you feel it's right! What is trending on Instagram is sharing the love by tagging others users. You could take advantage of this as an Instagram marketer, by tagging other companies, products, and other services on your post. You benefit from the means to not just draw traffic to your Instagram business profile but as well publicize your business on Instagram while helping other businesses.

The Use of Trending Hashtags and Emoji That Calls For Action

Instagram explore can be used to find trending hashtags/emoji that are related to the post you intend to make. Once you have found a hashtag or emoji relating to your post all you need to do is to put them in the caption area while posting.

When a user types one of the trending hashtag or emoji relating to the ones in your post, Instagram will automatically bring up your post as one of the suggestions. You could use both hashtags and emoji depending on whichever make more sense for your business. Before using this be sure that you're focused on how this can be channeled appropriately to your business.

Combination of Images and Videos

Combining pictures and videos is one of the best strategies to improve your Instagram marketing. Looking at the fact that videos are valuable tools in Instagram marketing by generating links. It helps increase the traffic and also increase your number of followers.

Instagram is all about telling stories, but you could bring this story to life by using some Instagram video editing tools. They are not just easy to create but also fun to use. All you need to do is press the record button and capture whatever you wish to advertise as part of your business, or you could just shoot a pre-made video. The main point is to make this video about the viewer's not just about the business alone.

Sponsor ads

Another aspect you need to consider as an Instagram marketer is sponsor ads. Sponsor ads occur on people's Instagram timeline regularly either one or multiple ads. This is a whole new view of your targeted audience, and it has the upper hand over any other method of marketing on Instagram.

People can only see the photos and videos of the Instagram account they follow, but with the sponsor ads, you would have reached a larger number of the Instagram users with the message you intend to pass across which helps you promote your business.

An Instagram marketer should have prepared contents that would be both engaging and as well created towards a demographic mind. You need to get some multiple posts ready to focus on different audiences.

Use Valuable Content

Instagram gives advertisers the opportunity to insert links that are clickable in their carousel posts. But, this URLs can't be clicked directly from the picture description. Using the link section of your Instagram account's bio, you can direct your followers to valuable contents on your website or blog.

Make sure that these posts are relevant to your audience. They are more willing to do what you ask if you are in touch with what they are thinking and feeling. Your posts need to reflect this.

Sponsor Post

Sponsor post helps to build massive exposure and audience. Instagram accounts with a large number of followers are available to render these services, so you need to find large accounts and pay for sponsored posts. It is cheapest of any ad platform now.

In fact, there are thousands of Instagram accounts built for just sponsored post alone and doing shout-outs to brands and companies. Most people run accounts with a significant amount of followers like this you just need to contact them to get started.

The sponsored posts will have to be submitted for review. There are certain requirements that will have to be met. When approved you will have the ability to reach thousands of users for a minimum number of dollars per day.

Boomerang

Boomerang is more GIF format than a photo app. With just a push of a button, the app takes a surge of photos and merge them together, creating a one-second video that plays both forward and backward continuously, either in portrait form or landscape form. It's all about engagement and being creative with the visual experience.

Having a boomerang to take some photos of your brand or business in a stylish and repetitive form will help strength your business. Although boomerang from Instagram is new, it does a great job in advertising your business on Instagram and any other social media network

Chapter 2

How to PROMOTE AND DRIVE SALES ON INSTAGRAM

Instagram marketers need to know that there are some ways to drive businesses on Instagram. While you are trying to grow your Instagram business profile you need to really focus on some primary aspects that would help promote your business on Instagram.

A Well-Branded Instagram Profile

The primary focus of people when they visit your Instagram profile is your Instagram feed. You would like to make an impression on your viewers, you need to make your Instagram feed not just about your business alone but also about the visitors.

Creating an awesome Instagram feed is not just about taking a lot of excellent pictures but it about making an impact on the sales. If you want to keep your Instagram profile more engaging to visitors, you need to post varieties of contents to aid consecutive visits. The mission is to create a balance with all post on Instagram feed.

Making a post of content related to your business is an excellent way to market your business on Instagram; it helps to educate more followers about your business.

Consistent Post

Regular posts on Instagram can engage more users and keep them updated about your business. This post need to be more intriguing, it has to be high-quality and actually passing the intended message across. An average Instagrammer posts at least once a day, but as an Instagram marketer that is looking to move your business to the next level with Instagram needs to post at least 3 times or more per day. If your posts get reposted on a regular basis and get engagements, then Instagram's algorithm would decide if your post should appear on top of your follower's feeds.

As far as when to post on Instagram, the best times are usually after 3pm during the week and to post often on the weekend. There are no "set" posting times that are optimal, but having an Instagram business profile and accessing the Insights tab will allow you to see what are the best times you get the most engagement.

Ask Your Followers to "Tag Other Friends."

You have just posted an Instagram photo or video about your business, and you need more engagement why not just edit the caption area and ask a friend to tag other friends. Using this most, you create more engagement on that post, thereby increasing the number of views on each post. This tactic works very well because when a friend tags another friend that the same friend could tag another friend growing the chain.

With the tactic implemented, the audience sees the engagement, making new followers more likely to engage and interact with your profile.

Learn to use the right filters

Knowing how to choose the right filter could help lead to more engagements and views on your Instagram feeds. Selecting filters is just fun because you get to see a different perspective in which your post could appear.

Researchers have discovered that using filters on your post gives a 21% viewing chance and 45% chance to be commented on than posting unfiltered contents. Filters get a high chance of views and comments.

According Bustle.com, photos with warmer filters tend to have higher engagement from different users. If you are looking to build the engagement, make sure to add the filters to your content, especially warmer color filters.

Be Responsive

The easiest way to keep this principle is to spend some time to just hang out with your Instagram followers by responding to comments and likes. You could even follow some new friends that have chosen to follow your page and make excellent comments on their post.

When making comments, be genuine. Have the other person feel like there is a real person behind the comments and likes. Too many times we get bombarded with generic comments, feeling as if whoever tried to engage was being transparent.

Spending the time to show love to your followers could actually bring the same back to you.

Driving Traffic from Instagram

Having to do the most challenges aspect on Instagram marketing by adding links to your bio for viewers to click and redirect. If you wish to direct your viewers to a particular link all you need do is to add a message to every post you make asking the view to visit your Instagram profile and go through the link in the bio.

The goal is to get as much traffic to your site. When creating the posts, create a Call to Action, telling the person that is viewing the photo or video to do something. It can be as simple as, "Click the Link in the Bio."

Exclusive Bonuses to Followers

Make your post more exciting with bonuses and special offers about your business. A study has shown that 41% of Instagrammers only follow or would follow a brand that gives bonuses and some other giveaways. Giving your followers this incentive you create more traffic from your Instagram thereby promoting your business. You can get third-party apps that can help to build text on photos you plan to post. Putting this text in a bold and large format; this will draw more attention towards your post.

To promote these sales and incentives, it would be a great idea to create a content calendar. The idea is to have a set amount of time and posting schedule so that the followers can take advantage of the opportunity.

Chapter 3.

Instagram Influencers (What Does This Mean?)

Instagram influencers can help you get massive traffic and engagement which will automatically bring high returns. Instagram influencer marketing is a perfect tool for an Instagram marketer in every aspect. Instagram marketers look up to another marketer to make their own purchase decisions. Influencers are intensely influenced by posts, likes and comments on Instagram and this way creating a new channel for businesses to endorse through other influential individuals.

Instagram influencer marketing is simply marketing brands, companies, businesses or services through other persons on Instagram who can influence their follower's decisions. Influencer marketing is similar to "word-of-mouth marketing," but it doesn't really recommend a lot of frank conversation. An influencer has the ability to sway consumers into taking prompt action.

In fact, for influencer marketing, Instagram has shown to be the best performing channel for social media work, with 3.21% engagement rate compared to other social media networks. Basically, with influencer marketing, you can identify relevant influencers who have a massive social following and get in touch them to see if they find interest in working with your business.

Benefits of Instagram Influencer

Help Improve Search Ranks

When you make an alliance with an Instagram influencer, you increase your chances of your brand being discovered. Keyword optimization alone can't have a weighty impact on your search rank.

Google only favors high-quality and organic links. Without having high-authority sites linked to you, you will have a hard time beating your competitors in the game, so you need an Instagram influencer on your side to help you beat the search engines at its game.

Engagement of New Audiences

Bonuses, contests, and giveaways are excellent ways to draw the attention of your audience. They also help you reach a set of new audiences relevant to your brand. With the audience feeling comfortable with the influencer, they will become comfortable with you once you associate your business to them.

Tips to Choosing An Instagram Influencer:

- **Find Top Influencers On Instagram:**
  You need to locate top influencers who already have their fans and already helped other companies become successful on Instagram. They can be a great way to promote your brand to the next level. It is necessary to build a great relationship with this Instagram influencer so that you don't need to change influencers all the time (that would be bad for business).

- **Find a niche that suits the season:**

It is important to find a niche that suits the season. Before you relate this niche to your influencer, you need to ask yourself, what kind of audience are you looking for? What kind of business are you planning to endorse? Understanding your niche helps you communicate the message better to your targeted audience.

- **Experiences with Brands**

  You need an influencer who treats themselves like the business and can understand you and what you want for your brand, taking to every instruction. Don't go for influencers that are all about money and sponsored contents alone.

- **Calculate Engagement Rate**

  How will you determine if an influencer is right for your business? It not just about how much followers an influencer has because sometimes follows can be faked on Instagram. But it is important to look at their feeds and know if their posts have a lot of engagement on it.

  You can use the process below to calculate the engagement rate of an influencer.

  You will need to create a spreadsheet and then list out all the links to each influencer you found, take record of some followers.

  Considering the number of followers should be a secondary option.

  Pick any three non-promotional photos that the influencer has posted on Instagram, you need to note the number of comments and likes on this pictures.

  Calculate the person engagement rate for each picture with this formula below.

  $A = $ (number of likes $+$ number of comments) / number of followers

  $E = (A+B+C)/3$

  $E = $ Post Engagement Rate

  $A = $ Engagement Rate for Image 1

  $B = $ Engagement Rate for Image 2

  $C = $ Engagement Rate for Image 3

Take a look at the average of three different posts to determine the final post of the influencer.
The highest engagement tells you which influencer is stronger and has a wider reach.

- **Building a Solid Relationship with Influencer**
Before you think of talking to an influencer about partnership.it is necessary to build a relationship with them thereby letting them know you are real and ready to work with them. Show how much interest you have in cooperating with them.

  After establishing a perfect relationship with your influencers start asking for a partnership to work together. Your statement should outline the essential details of the kind of work you expect from them and what you intend achieving with your partnership.

YOUTUBE MARKETING

HOW TO USE VIDEO MARKETING TO PROMOTE YOUR BUSINESS

By

HARWOOD E. JONES

Copyright © 2017

Email: midnightmediallc@gmail.com

Website: Midnight Media

Table of Contents

Introduction to YouTube 84

IDENTIFY YOUR TARGET AUDIENCE88

CREATE ORIGINAL 90

CONTENT ON A....................................90

REGULAR BASIS. 90

FOLLOWING THE....................................93

EXAMPLES SET BY COMPANIES WITH ESTABLISHED POPULAR YOUTUBE CHANNELS.......93

RELATIVITY (Make your channel content relative to your viewers).......................................96

SUPPORT CUSTOMER RESEARCH WITH KEYWORDS 98

SET A BUDGET 100

PROMOTION IS KEY 102

About The Author...........................104

Other Books By Harwood Jones 105

Can I Ask a Favor? 106

Introduction to YouTube

YouTube is the 2nd most popular searched site on the Internet after Google. With over 150 million videos watched daily, it is easy to see why YouTube is the ultimate avenue to market your business, product or idea on. Definitely the biggest pool of potential customers you can reach for free.

YouTube's theme is "Broadcast Yourself", so marketing your brand is encouraged and definitely a good idea for your brand. YouTube is owned by Google and leverages the search power of Google. Using YouTube for marketing is not utilized enough by business owners and entrepreneurs alike.

If you want to succeed in 2017

you need to come to this simple realization:

Printed Media and

Print Media can only reach a

limited amount of potential customers and frankly a dying medium.

You need to market your business online and paperless.

Whether it's YouTube, Pinterest, Facebook, Twitter, Craig's List and other popular social media outlets, you need to get your message across the board to optimize your brand and reach thousands online in a very short amount of time.

Creating an account and simply posting one marketing video will not leave any lasting impression. You have to keep your YouTube channel evolving and relevant.

Build an audience into your marketing effort in order to increase your ranking and reach even more potential customers.

In this book our goal is to give you the essential steps to successfully marketing your brand and reaching your target audience.

Whether you want to get noticed on the internet or use your YouTube channel to make money and earn a living, first thing you'll need is a Google email address to get the process started smoothly. Channel art is another important factor to get noticed.

The channel description needs to be planned, and use Google to see examples of channel descriptions that are suggested by experienced YouTube broadcasters.

Develop content that is going to catch the viewers eye and attention. Now that you have a viewer hooked you have to actively promote your channel in order to rise up the rankings and gain popularity.

Know you might ask what exactly is channel art? Channel art is the image that is seen at the very top of your page also known as your cover image. This Image will have to draw your viewer's attention.

The recommended image dimensions are **2560 x 1440 pixels**. Change this cover image on a regular basis.

Make sure to include your channel name the product or service you have to offer and your logo in the channel art.

This helps the viewer recognize your brand in the future creating brand awareness. Now that you have addressed the cover art portion of your channel the next step would be to come up with a description for your YouTube channel.

This brief description should include links to other websites, your product, services, or examples of services rendered.

Naming your YouTube channel is your next move. If you're a business looking to advertise your product/services on YouTube, its best to have your company name as the name of your YouTube channel.

However, this is not set in stone. Another approach could be to look at your description and video content and use these parameters to determine your name.

There is no concrete way to insure success simply by the name. You must just come up with a name that is memorable.

Here we have just gone over the basic starting points of the creation of a YouTube channel. From here we will walk through the process of promoting and growing your channel to a wider audience.

We have broken it down to 7 steps that will promote your business using YouTube.

Use the information to build brand and authority and to put yourself in the best position to grow your business.

IDENTIFY YOUR TARGET AUDIENCE

It is crucial that you identify your target audience. Who exactly are you trying to sell your brand too? Tailor your content to reach that audience.

Every audience is different. Your job is to learn how to reach them and make your channel unique and stand out clearly. If you create good enough material that you have an audience who checks your YouTube channel daily, your channel can be considered a success. You may ask "How do I reach my target audience?"

Before you can answer that question there are a couple key checks you need to make.

- "Are you selling something, are you building exposure or are you trying to promote something?
- Who is the YouTube channel for?
- How are you going to deliver them?

If you are not a creative person, and you doubt you can bring your vision for your YouTube channel to life, you should consider getting help or outsourcing the building process to someone qualified online.

For example, let's say your business is a Women's Clothing Store.

Your YouTube should be a Fashion driven channel and preferably hosted as a young woman with a keen sense of fashion and everything fashion related.

You need someone with charisma and flair to capture your target audience and bring them back on a daily basis.

Viewers determine a video's worth within the first 5 seconds. Strive to make your first 5 seconds entertaining. I know that sounds impossible, but it's the small window you have to work with.

Teaser clips are another way to keep a viewer locked onto you channel.

These may be shorter clips that get your audience excited and curious about what you have to say and or offer. The goal is to build curiosity while fulfilling what your audience wants to consume.

Your video needs to be an entertaining story or an informative interesting flow of facts and figures. These facts need to be relevant to how the audience is feeling about relevant problems they see. They look to your channel for answers and you need to be able to solve the problems your audience has. This will build the trust factor, and they will continue to hear from you.

CREATE ORIGINAL CONTENT ON A REGULAR BASIS.

Your channel needs to be entertaining and original. You want to captivate your target audience and you want new videos on your channel on a regular basis.

One pitfall to look out for is lowering the quality of your channel. By quality we mean producing videos that have been constructed with a plan in place. Ideally you want to have an idea of what will be talked about and must be relevant. However, don't worry too much on producing George Lucas quality. Just create originals.

You do want to keep the same idea of content, but you don't want it to become repetitive. Mix it up from time to time. Change settings and set ups until you have a feel of what you want your content to be like.

Using tools like annotations are a good idea. Annotations are text placeholder boxes that appear in your video stream.

They can be used to emphasize certain points in your video, promote products or websites and more. A good one to end your video with is an annotation reminding the viewer to subscribe to your channel. Your video needs to be an entertaining story or an informative interesting flow of facts and figures.

Long videos need to be broke down to its most condensed form without losing any substance. This make the content more digestible and your viewer will remember more of the message or brand you trying to portray.

Overloading your channel with sub par videos in an attempt to have new content on your channel is not a good idea.

Content quality is crucial. Find subtle ways to put your product/services in the video without the viewer getting bored. Entertaining viewers leads to more people subscribing which is what you you want. Additionally, you will have videos that for one or other reason will not be as popular as other videos on your channel.

The key is to have the popular videos highlighted in your News Feed, making it the first thing new visitors to your channel see.

Adding content is your bread and butter. Making an error here could make or break your channel. Look at what's out there, study your direct competition, and offer something better to viewers.

The general public uses YouTube for a variety of things from watching cat videos, learning to cook fine French cuisine, laughing at stand up comics and learning how to create a WordPress website.

Now think about what you bring to the audience and how you can stand out from the thousands of YouTube channels already out there.

What exactly is your strengths and what can you offer the world? This is a fundamental question. And I can not emphasize this enough, "You will have to keep your viewers coming back for more."

The best thing to do is a little research. Find other YouTube channels you like and look for elements you would like to recreate. The idea is not to copy, but to make it your own.

When starting out having a little experience with filming videos goes a long way, but not necessarily the most important. Practice and hone your skills until you are proficient and you produce quality content.

Brush up your skills constantly and have the right equipment, a tripod will become your best friend because there is nothing worse than a shaky video.

Editing videos will make stronger impressions and give your viewers the impression that you know what you are doing. There are thousands of instructional and tutorial videos on YouTube that you can utilize to improve your channel.

Even standard video editing software is more than adequate to make and edit your videos.

There is also a lot of online resources you can use as well.

And even for the newest of YouTubers, the emphasis is just to start. With the quality of current smartphones, these are good enough to film with. It's always on you and is ready at a moments notice. Just create content as often as possible.

FOLLOWING THE

EXAMPLES SET BY COMPANIES WITH ESTABLISHED POPULAR YOUTUBE CHANNELS

Some companies are knocking it out of the park when it comes to marketing strategies and getting their brand presence out to millions of viewers across the globe. Studies show that watching a video is one of the most common activities by smartphone users. Your video presence on YouTube is a direct reflection of your company and your brand.

Here are a couple of Titans of YouTube Marketing you should study and learn from. Sure you do not have the same financial resources or manpower theses giants of industries but there is a lot your can learn from them.

Red Bull

The energy drink phenom has over 4 million subscribers on their channel. They reached a billion views in it's first 6 years. Their videos are full of amazing people doing pretty amazing things. Parkour, cliff diving and driving a race car on ice. **Key Takeaway: Embody the lifestyle that your customer would have after using your product or service.**

Walmart

Walmart, hate it or love it, but the Retail Giant knows how to market on YouTube. With a massive variety of videos on their channel ranging from D.I.Y. videos to easy cooking video recipes to keep their audience engaged.

A wide variety of quality video content gives viewers a lot more options to view and allows them to stay on your channel longer in turn exposing them longer to your product and marketing campaign.

Key Takeaway: Use variety in your own content.

PlayStation

One of the 10 best branded channels on YouTube and it is no surprise the Japanese Gaming Mogul is leaps and bounds ahead in its marketing campaigns on YouTube compared to their closest rivals.

With over 3500 videos uploaded and millions of subscribers one thing Sony PlayStation has done incredibly well is include its logo on the bottom left corner of the videos.

Key Takeaway: Company branding in your content is crucial and a great tool to increase brand visibility.

EQUALS 3 (Ray William Johnson)

If you do not know who Ray William Johnson is, you have been stuck under a rock somewhere or you have never been on YouTube.

Ray is an American actor, comedian who started a YouTube channel web series called Equals 3. From humble beginnings, Ray has grown the channel to nearly 3 billion views and 10 million subscribers in 2015, making it one of the most successful YouTube channels of all time. Johnson started to branch out into other mediums and he owns his own lucrative production company these days as well.

This proves that your possibilities on YouTube are endless, and it all started from one YouTube channel. Ray's comedic delivery and trending compilation videos is the keys to his success.

Key takeaway: Entertain your audience, branding should be a secondary goal. Your first and only goal at first is to captivate your viewers, the rest will follow.

RELATIVITY (Make your channel content relative to your viewers)

Viewers want to watch videos they can relate to in one or other way. Overt marketing strategies like television commercials still have a place in the marketing spectrum, but relating to your viewers on a personal level leaves a lasting impression on them.

There are various examples on YouTube where companies used this principle exceptionally.

Nike (Margot vs Lilly)

In trying to improve the business amongst women, the sportswear giant produced this web series focusing on two sisters who make an unusual bet with each other.

The videos focus on a clear athletic focus and Nike scattered throughout the background.

But the crucial element in the campaign is the story told brilliantly over the eight-part series, without forcing their product down the consumers. Nike reached millions of consumer worldwide with this creative web series.

Purina (Puppy hood)

Purina's "Puppy Hood" campaign is another excellent example of relating to their consumer by providing them with adorable puppies in their videos.

Who doesn't like puppy videos?

The web series follows a man who decides to adopt a puppy. The relationship between the man and his new best friend leaves every person who ever owned a dog to relate and have an emotional attachment.

With over 15 million views you can't deny that by pulling one the viewers heart strings isn't what has grown this channel.

Another classic example of relating to the viewer, "Puppy Hood" was a marketing home run if I have ever seen one.

SUPPORT CUSTOMER RESEARCH WITH KEYWORDS

Consider words and phrases that are relevant to both your product and industry. Your keywords need to be regularly searched words. YouTube provides rankings of the most searched keywords on their platform this an important tool to use when selling up your channel and uploading a new video.

There are multiple ways to conduct keyword research for your videos. One of the simplest ways is to go on YouTube and insert a search. When inputting keywords, look at how certain phrases automatically come up. These are words and phrases most searched by users and are key indicators these are the types of videos people are searching for.

Another way is to look up Google Trends. Look for topics that are currently popular and being searched on the internet. Make your videos relevant to these current events.

One other way that may be of use is to use Google AdWords Keyword Planner. It can only be accessed by creating an AdWords account. If you choose to go this route you will have to create an AdWords campaign, but pause it from going live, and you will have access to the dashboard.

Use the Keyword Planner to see what keywords associated with your product or service is being most researched. From there you can use these keywords when creating your videos since they will appear in Google search results.

SET A BUDGET

The cost per view charged for YouTube sponsorships varies widely. Depending on reach, demographics, engagement, audience size and genre.

Rule to abide by is to target 0.07cents cost per view (CPV) for video integrations and a 0.10cents CPV for dedicated videos. Start small with your set up criteria selections.

Grow your online persona first before expanding your demographic and reach.

This is a key component in the early life span of your marketing campaign and should not be rushed or overlooked.

A poor budget and finance allocation can ruin a promising marketing campaign before it even starts. Make sure you have a way to make money from your campaign.

Whether you marketing for an affiliate marketer promoting a product for a commission or marketing your own product or services be sure you have a plan for monetizing the traffic you can receive from YouTube.

Success on YouTube requires dedication and patience. Be consistent and stick with it. You never when your videos will "pop" and gain instant success and explode on the internet. Continue to put out high quality content and get people to continue watching.

PROMOTION IS KEY

Promote your channel effectively in order to separate yourself from the crowd. Start with the title, a great title is the first thing a viewer sees when it comes across your content on YouTube.

Keep it short and to the point. A great title is essential to get viewers through the door.

Your video thumbnail is another important part of the promotion process. Needs to be clear, use a large quality image because it will be used as the preview in the embedded player.

Interaction with your viewers is very important and responding to your viewers' comments will go a long time. This way you build a connection with your viewers that goes a long way.

Posting questions to your viewers will help gain regular viewers.

You will come across a couple trolls who go out of their way to abuse other users in your comment thread and do all they can to get under your skin.

Best to just remove their comments off the thread and focus all your attention on the positive viewers on your comment thread. Doing reviews are a brilliant way to also gain loyal subscribers.

Channel defaults settings can help increase your channel's consistency and boost you video in the YouTube algorithm.

If you have made a name for yourself posting random funny compilation videos, spend an episode talking directly with the audience, answering popular questions from the comments and discussing the process of your creativity.

This behind-the-scenes access goes a long way with viewers.

During big calendar events and holidays, increase the amount of content you release to continue capitalizing on new viewers.

More content shows viewers that you are knowledgeable and passionate about the occasion.

Remember it's also important to promote your channel as much offline as it is online. Tell your family, friends, coworkers, and let them know about your channel. They may find the information relevant and share with their other friends and people they interact with.

Promote across all mediums so that everyone is updated on new videos. Remember to be consistent and relevant.

About The Author

Harwood Jones is the CEO and Founder of Midnight Media, LLC in Metairie, Louisiana, specializing in digital and social media marketing. By day, he can be found in the classroom, teaching Business Computer Applications and serving as the Head of the Business Department. You can find him here growing his audience on YouTube, sharing his insights on all things marketing and social media.